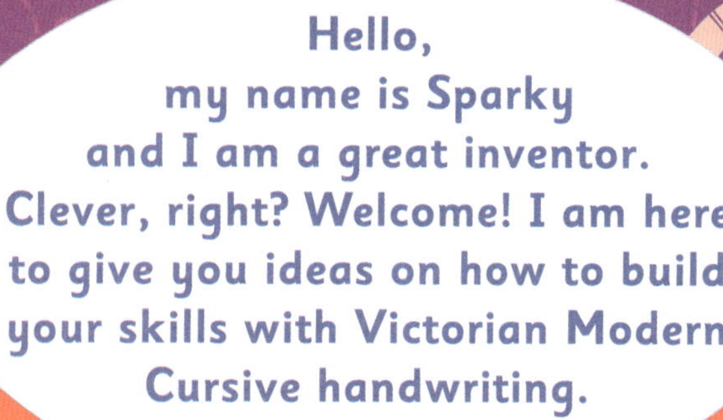

My inventor's profile

Name: ______________________

Class: ____________ Birthday: ____________

Place of birth: ______________________

Two interesting facts about me:

1. ______________________

2. ______________________

Three things I'd like to invent:

1. ______________________

2. ______________________

3. ______________________

My progress passport

Inventors and innovators come from all over the world! Some of the most important inventions came from Africa and Asia (such as pottery, the wheel, glass and paper), but they were so long ago that we don't know the names of the individual inventors. This is equally true of the First Nations Australians who invented many items and continue to develop practices that show both resourcefulness and a great knowledge of science.

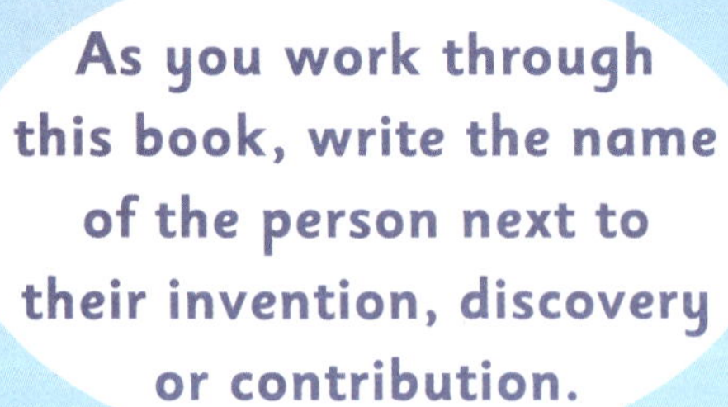

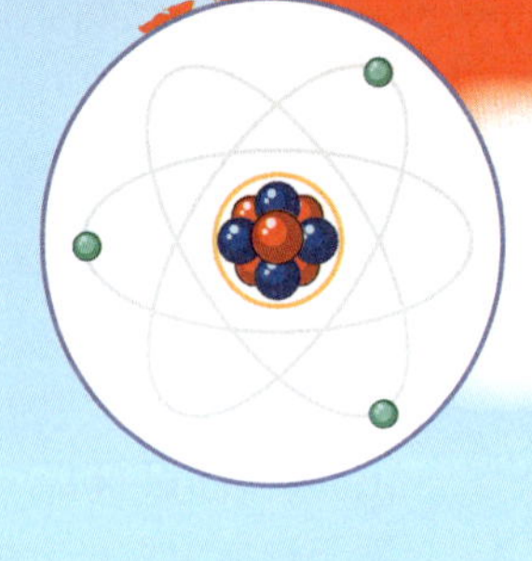

Look for this icon to find the right name.

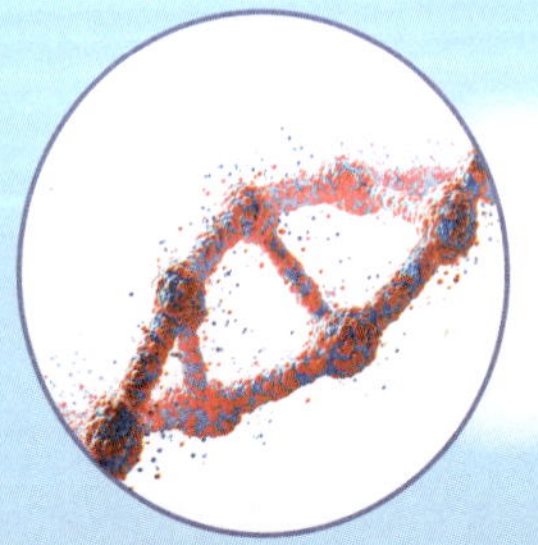

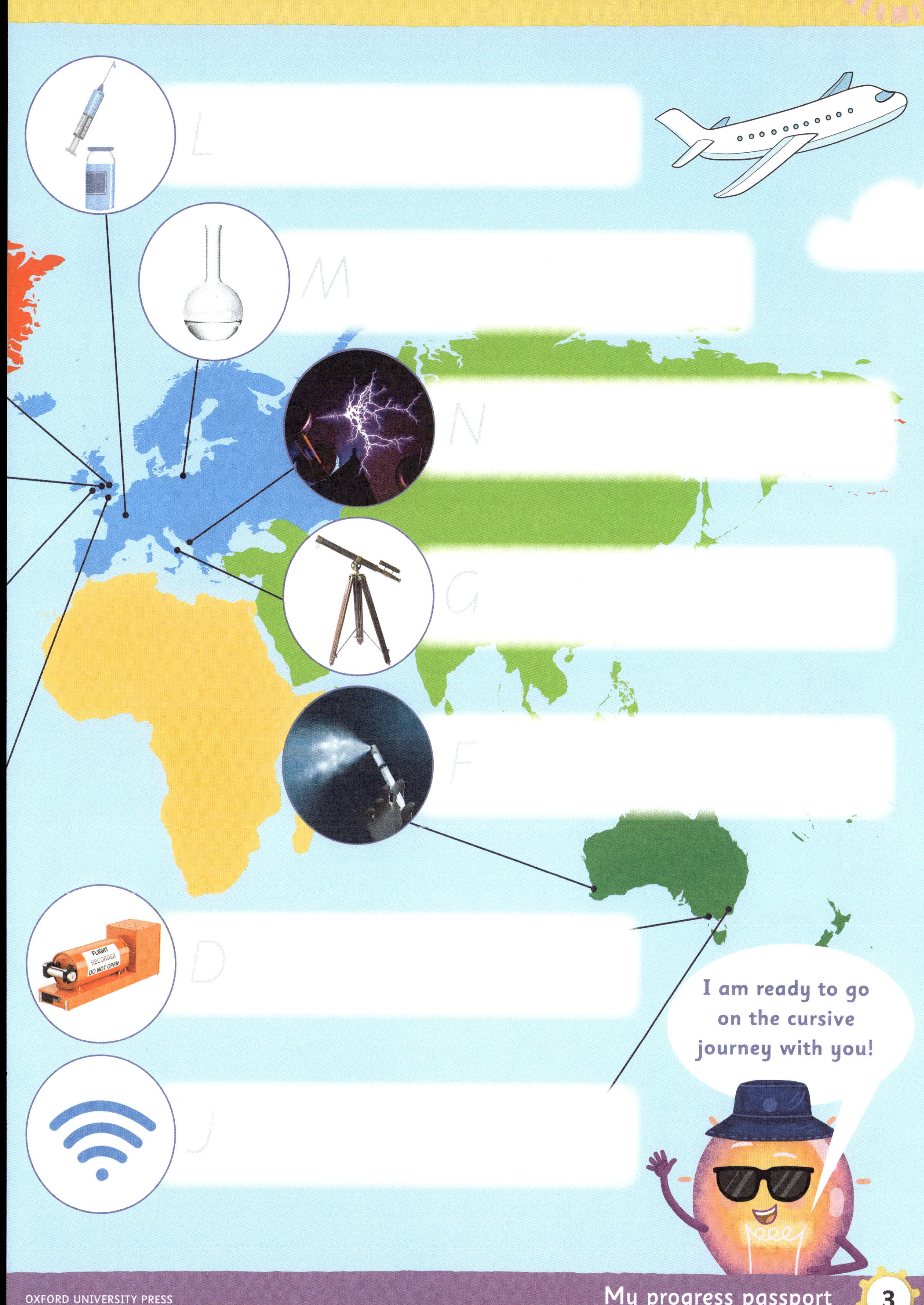
L
M
N
G
F
FLIGHT
RECORDER
DO NOT OPEN
D
J
I am ready to go on the cursive journey with you!

Before you begin writing ...

Here are the 3Ps that will help you with your writing: posture, pencil/pen grip and paper position. You will be reminded about these as you work through the book.

Posture

Relax your arms and make sure the chair supports your back. Check that your feet are flat on the floor.

Pencil/pen grip

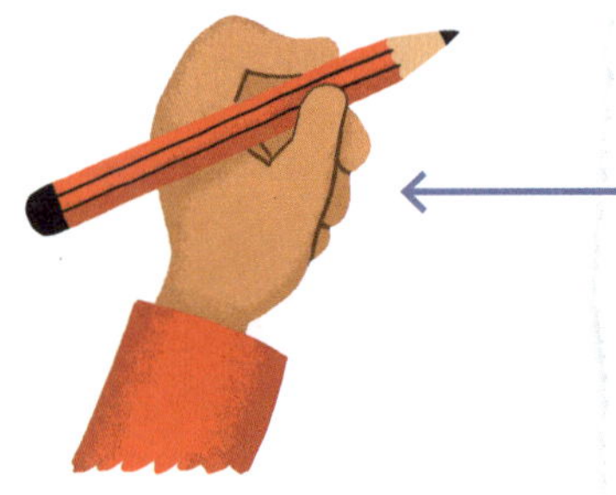

Left-handed

How you hold your pencil/pen is most important. Hold your pencil/pen firmly between your thumb and index finger, balanced on your middle fingers (2.5 cm before the end and not too tightly!).

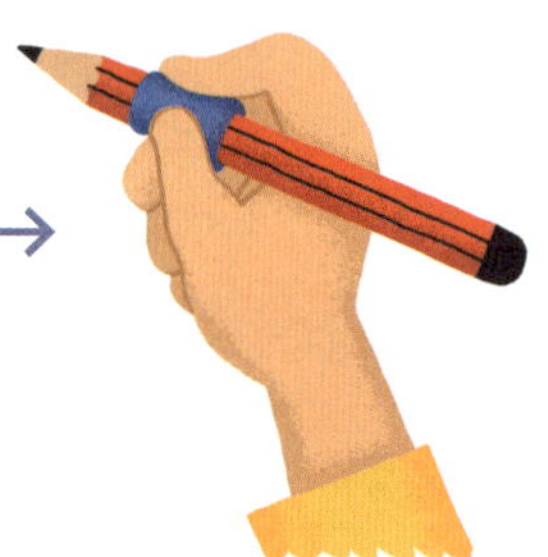

Right-handed

Paper position

Left-handed

Angle your page and use your non-writing hand to steady the page.

Right-handed

Left-handers may form some letters differently. For example, for the capital letters A, E, F, H, T, the left-handed person might go from right to left to make the join:

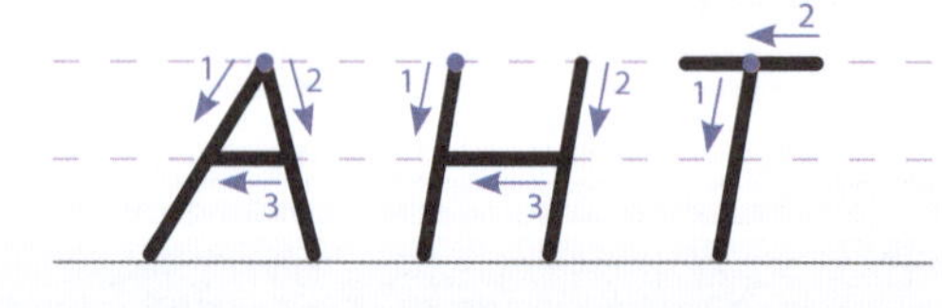

Revision

Victorian Modern Cursive print

Learning intention:
To revise Victorian Modern Cursive print handwriting

Trace these letters, punctuation marks and numbers.

aA bB cC dD eE fF gG hH

iI jJ kK lL mM nN oO pP

qQ rR sS tT uU vV wW xX

yY zZ . , " " ' ? ! ; :

0 1 2 3 4 5 6 7 8 9 10

Copy the names of these countries. Link the capital letter to the matching lower case letter or letters in that word, for example, Australia.

Australia Albania Barbados

Eritrea Timor-Leste Uruguay

Fluency patterns

Learning intention: To practise my fluency joins

Tip!

Take your time here to practise your fluency joins. Getting this right will help you throughout your cursive handwriting journey.

Copy these fluency patterns.

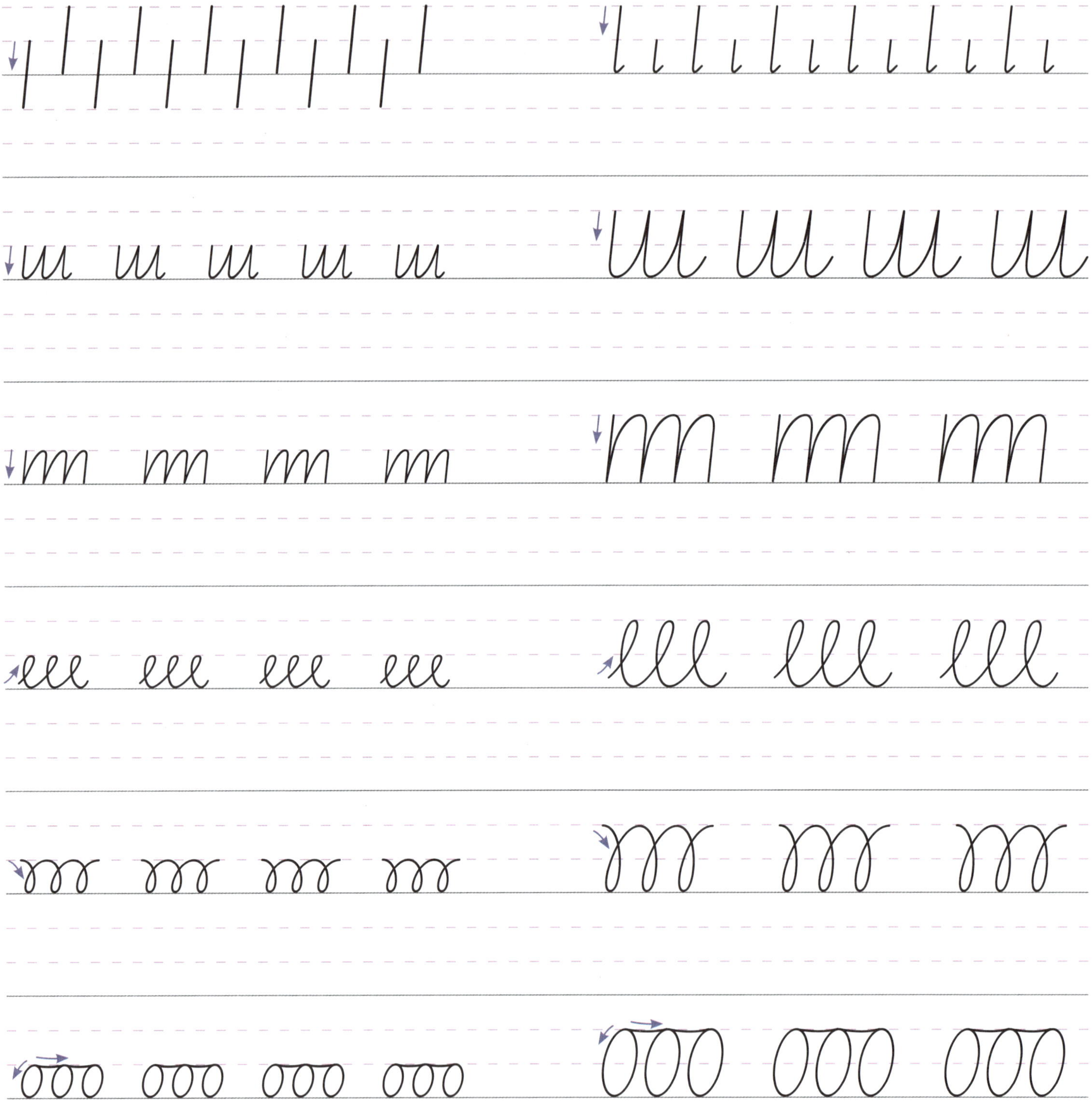

OXFORD UNIVERSITY PRESS

Copy these patterns.

Self-assessment Draw a heart on top of your neatest three patterns.

Diagonal joins

Learning intention:
To revise letters with a diagonal join

Tip!

We know a diagonal join goes from one letter's exit flick up to meet the next letter. Practise the diagonal joins below. Remember, the pencil/pen stays on the paper.

Trace and then copy these diagonal joins.

ai am an ap ar au ay

ce cu cy de di du dy

en ey he hu pi xe xt

Copy this sentence to practise your diagonal joins.

Creativity shapes our world.

Diagonal joins to tall letters

Learning intention:
To use diagonal joins with tall letters

this ✓

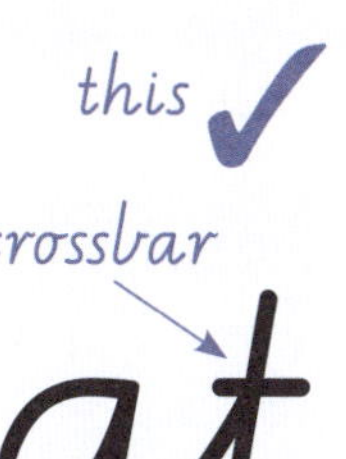

not this ✗

at

Tip! Remember that the top of the t starts above the middle line. Then we add the crossbar last.

Trace and then copy these diagonal joins.

at af ah ak al at ct

ef ek el et ib if it

ub ut uk ub uh ul ut

Copy this sentence to practise your diagonal joins.

Put on your imaginary inventor's hat to make history!

Drop-in joins

Learning intention:
To write letters that are dropped into place with a drop-in join

When we join to anti-clockwise letters (such as a, c, d, g and q), the exit from the first letter reaches high towards the top of the anti-clockwise letter.

The a touches the exit here.

Trace and then copy these drop-in joins for a, c, d, g and q.

la ia ha ac ec uc ed id ld

ag ma ig aq eq ng ca ud nq

Trace and then copy these words, which include letters with drop-in joins.

Alexander Graham Bell invented

the telephone in 1876.

Horizontal joins

Learning intention:

To write letters with horizontal joins

Tip! The horizontal join for b, o, r, v and w has a slight dip. The horizontal join for f is straight. Use the crossbar from f to join to the next letter.

slight dip

ba fi on ri vu wi

Trace and then copy these horizontal joins.

be bl bi br bu fi fu fy

oi om on op or ou ov oy

ri rm rn rp rr ru rv ry

vi vu vv vy vi vu vv vy

wi wm wn wr wy wi wr

Horizontal joins to anti-clockwise letters

Learning intention:
To write anti-clockwise letters with horizontal joins

Tip! When writing horizontal joins to anti-clockwise letters, go across to the start of the letter, then **retrace**.

oa

Trace and then copy these letter pairs and words.

ba bo oa oc oo og os od oa oc oo

ra rc ro rg rs rd ba bc bd

wa wc wo fa fo fc va vo

vacuum waves vibrations radio

locomotive phonograph aeroplane

Horizontal joins to tall letters

Learning intention:
To join short letters to tall letters

Tip!

When you make a join to tall letters, go right to the top and then retrace a little as you move downwards.

Trace and then copy these letter pairs.

ol ob oh ol ok ob

rl rk rt rb rh rt rl

wk wh wl wt vl vt vk vh

Teacher comment

Letters that do not join

Learning intention:
To write letters that have clockwise finishers

Tip! Letters that finish in a clockwise direction do not join.

g j y z

Trace and then copy these letters that finish in a clockwise direction.

g j y z

Copy these letter pairs and words on the lines below.

ga gave go goal gu gusty

ja jargon ji jigsaw jo joke

ye yes yo yoghurt yu yummy

ze zest zi zippy zo zoo

Capital letters

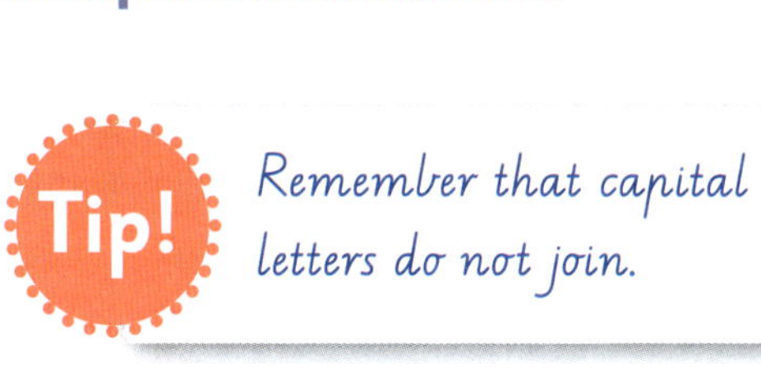

Learning intention:
To write words with capital letters

Trace and then copy these capital letters.

A B C D E F G

H I J K L M N

O P Q R S T U

V W X Y Z

Copy these place names.

Melbourne Victoria Australia

Copy the sentence below, which includes letters that do and do not join.

James Chadwick was an English physicist. He proved the existence of neutrons, for which he received the Nobel Prize in Physics in 1935.

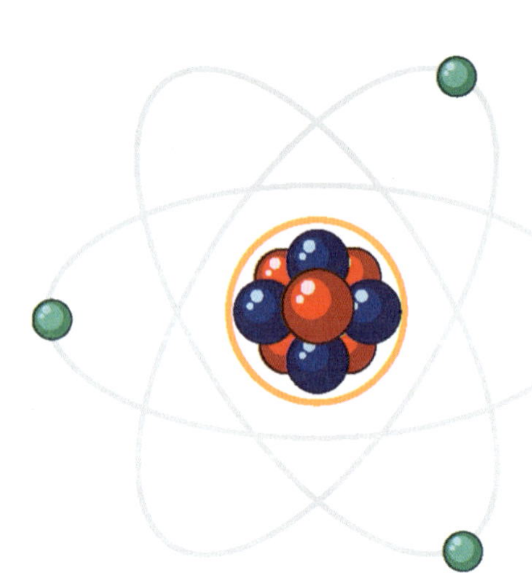

Self-assessment

Assess how you are going with letters that do not join.

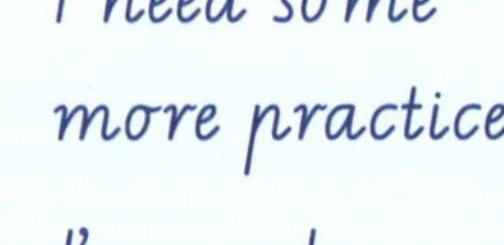

❑ I need some more practice

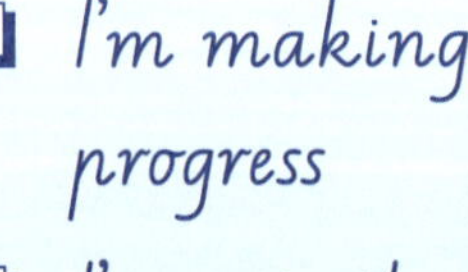

❑ I'm making progress

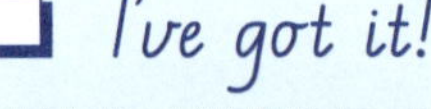

❑ I've got it!

Teacher comment

Joins from q to u

qu

The diagonal join is very long.

Trace and then copy these letter pairs with qu joins.

qu qu qu qu qu qu qu

Copy these words and then draw a line to match each word to its picture. The first one is done for you.

queen quilt quiet quick quokka

queen

Consolidating

Learning intention:
To review my print handwriting

Tip! Remember to always use printing for the labels on maps and diagrams.

Label the diagram with the words at the bottom of the page. Use print handwriting. One is done for you.

power switch

This older computer looks different from a laptop or tablet, but you can see how they have some of the same features.

monitor hard drive keyboard mouse
~~power switch~~ CD drive USB port

Assessment: All joins

I am successful when I can:

- ❏ check my 3Ps
- ❏ write letters that contain joins.

With a coloured pencil, shade the letter pairs that would have a diagonal join.

mp	Fa	al	xy	fi
ac	pe	Lm	ox	om
be	ng	cr	Ja	oh
hi	or	de	po	rk

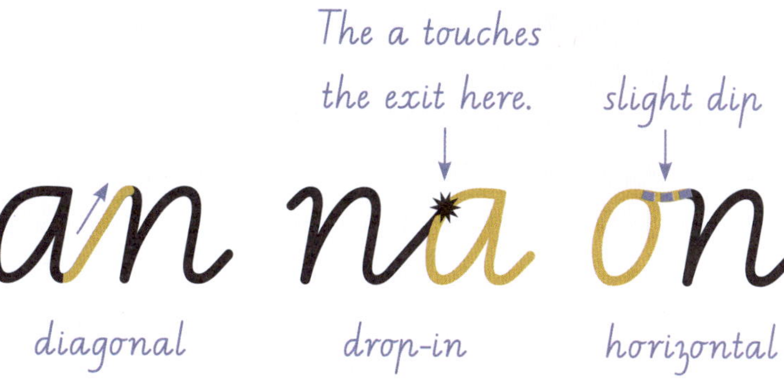

With a coloured pencil, shade the letter pairs that would have a horizontal join.

mp	Fa	al	xy	fi
ac	pe	Lm	ox	om
be	ng	cr	Ja	oh
hi	or	de	po	rk

With a coloured pencil, shade the letter pairs that would have a drop-in join.

mp	Fa	al	xy	fi
ac	pe	Lm	ox	om
be	ng	cr	Ja	oh
hi	or	de	po	rk

Self-assessment

Assess how you are going with all joins.

❏ I need some more practice

❏ I'm making progress

❏ I've got it!

Teacher comment

Smaller lines

Writing on smaller lines

Learning intention:
To write Victorian Modern Cursive handwriting on smaller lines

Did you know that if you could travel as fast as light, the universe would look very different?

Well, I don't expect you to travel at the speed of light, but writing on smaller lines will help you write faster!

Copy these sentences to practise writing on smaller lines.

To help make your writing a little faster,

we will practise writing on smaller lines.

Check your 3Ps and then copy these

sentences in your neatest handwriting.

Check over your work.

Self-assessment Circle your neatest three words!

Tricky joins

Joins to s

Tip! We can use horizontal joins to connect letters to s. This requires some retracing at the top. Go across to form the top of the s, then retrace the top on your way down.

Trace these horizontal joins to s. Then use a coloured pencil to colour where you retraced the letter s.

bs os rs ws fs

bs os rs ws fs

Trace and then copy these words.

loss first flowers position chefs claws

screws closer verse swimmers boost

carriers absorption observe atmosphere

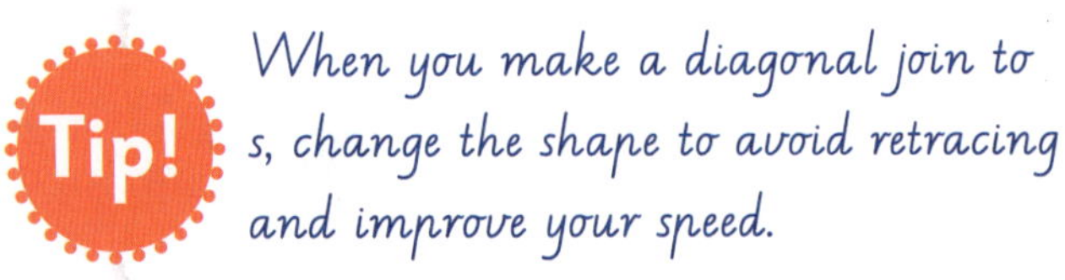

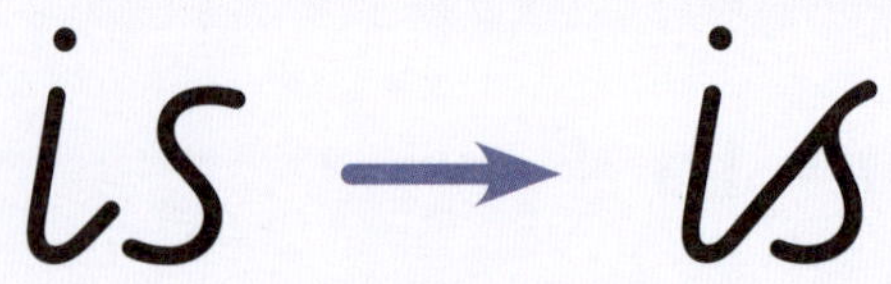

Trace and then copy these letter pairs to practise diagonal joins to s.

ps xs es ts cs ds is ks

as cs ds es hs is ks ls

Trace and then copy these words.

atoms beams optics myths

aeons gadgets scissors screws

his past videos wheelbarrows

hands best last this cakes music

fashion physics invents myths

Trace and then copy these sentences.

New innovations in technology help us do things in an easier, quicker and more accurate way.

What innovation or invention would you like to see? Would you like to travel quickly between countries or help cure a sickness?

Draw a picture of your innovation or invention!

Joins to e

Learning intention: To write a join to e

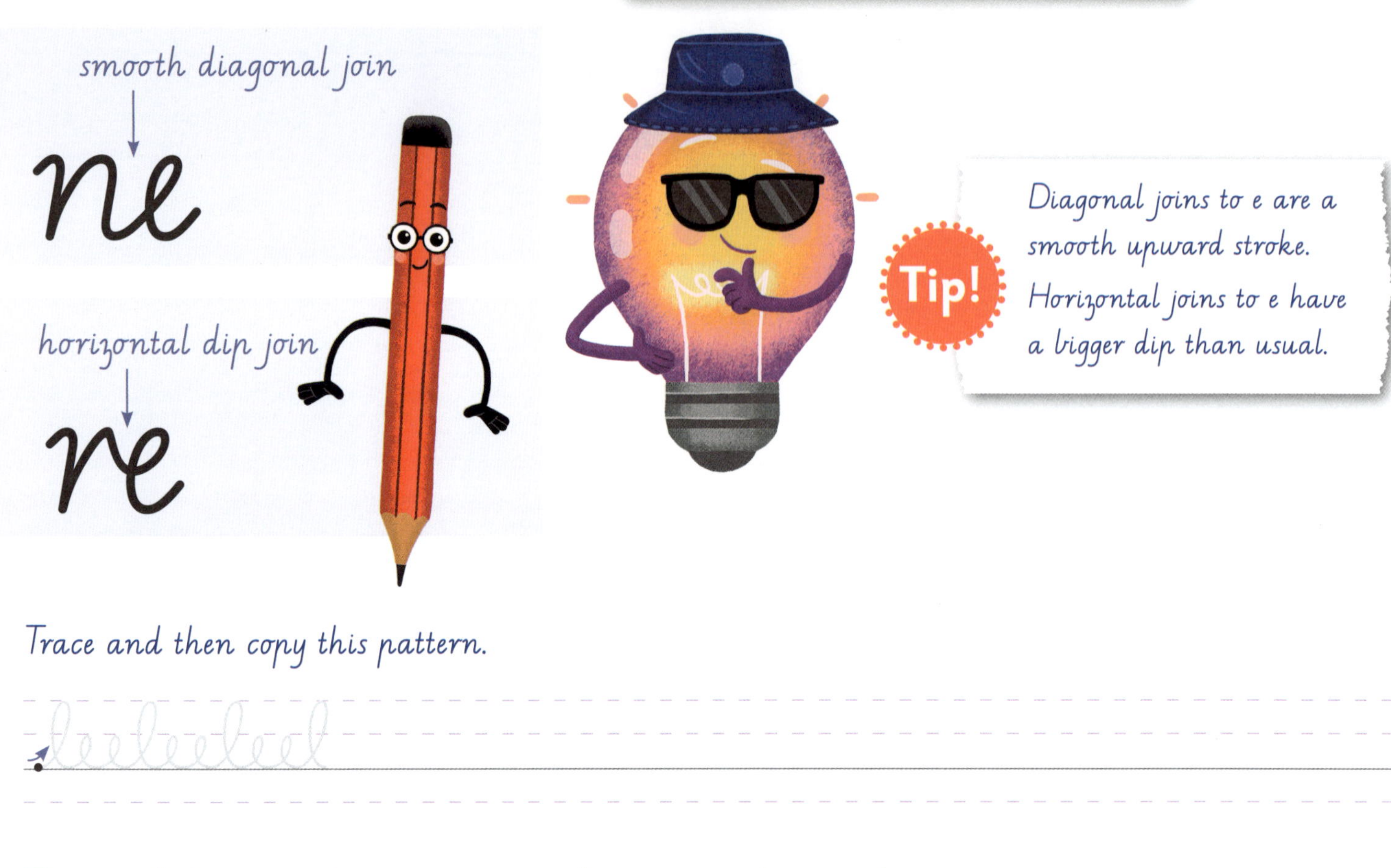

Trace and then copy this pattern.

eeleeleel

Trace and then copy these joins to e in the space on the same line.

oe re ve we xe

Trace and then copy these words.

poems whichever save taxes

core believe travel before

stare weather canoe

Joins to f

Learning intention:
To practise the looped f

Tip!

Diagonal joins to f swing up to form a small loop. The loop crosses at the same height as body letters.

The letter f at the beginning of a word or after a pencil lift looks like this: f

When letters join to f it is written like this: f

Use a diagonal join to practise these joins to f.

af ef if uf lf af ef if uf lf

calf sniff before raffle life puff

yourself reef strife

unify whiff afloat

Did you know?
Rosalind Franklin created the first X-ray picture of DNA, called Photo 51, which helped lead to the discovery of the molecular structure of DNA.

Self-assessment

Draw a star on your neatest three joins to f.

I am successful when I can:

- [ ] add a horizontal join to f.

of rf wf xf of rf wf of rf

coffee colourful lawful sofa

scarf surf Oxford snowfall

Copy this sentence.

Ms Orfanos fished for five

hours at the surf beach.

Trace and then copy these words with joins to and from the letter f.

waterfall different follow forest after

lift fiftieth fishing fixed magnify

Joins to z

Learning intention: *To join letters to the letter z*

Diagonal joins to z swing up to meet the start of the letter. The horizontal joins swing across smoothly to the top of the letter.

Trace and then copy these words to practise your joins to z.

amazing breeze size prizes

frozen puzzles doze dozen

Joins to and from x

Learning intention: *To join letters to and from the letter x*

slight dip

Diagonal joins to x swing around in a clockwise direction, then you lift your pen or pencil to form the anti-clockwise part. When you do a horizontal join, add a slight dip.

Trace and then copy these words to practise your joins to and from x.

excitement exploration excellence

fix box extra exercise fox toxic

example exact expand expert

Consolidating

Learning intention:
To review all I have learnt with cursive handwriting

Copy these sentences.

Cameras used to be heavy, bulky and awkward to handle. They were very sensitive to changes in light levels, and any shaking would blur the photo. These days, cameras are small, portable and can even be used underwater.

OXFORD UNIVERSITY PRESS

Copy these sentences.

Did you know that the technology to create wireless networks was invented in Australia? In 1992, Dr John O'Sullivan and the CSIRO developed technology to reduce the echo of radio waves, which allows wifi to work. It is now used by billions of people and has changed the way we live.

Assessment: Tricky joins

Copy this selection of inventions. With a coloured pencil, go over any drop-in, horizontal or diagonal joins.

telephone typewriter handwriting compass

fruit peeler sponge battery kettle computer

sewing machine alarm clock black box

Complete the sentence below.

My favourite invention is ______________________

because ______________________

____

____

______________________.

Self-assessment

Assess how you are going with tricky joins.

❑ I need some more practice

❑ I'm making progress

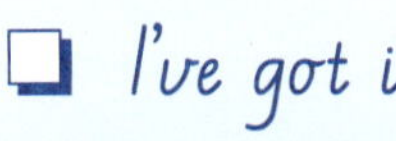

❑ I've got it!

Teacher comment

More tricky joins

Practising tricky joins

Copy the sentences below to practise your tricky joins.

Italian astronomer and mathematician,

Galileo Galilei is known as the father of

modern astronomy and physics. He lived

from 1564 to 1642. His improvements to

the telescope led to key

astronomical discoveries,

including that the Earth

revolves around the Sun.

The letter f

f at the start of a word → function

craft ← f within a word

Copy these sentences.

Darri saw some flying fish flip, flop, flap and float in the air. She wondered if these fish had inspired Leonardo da Vinci to envisage a flying machine, which he did many drawings of.

She resolved to look this up when she got back home.

OXFORD UNIVERSITY PRESS

Double letters

Learning intention:

To practise letter pairs and words with double letters

Make sure your double letters are not too far apart. Writing the double f, the crossbar on the first f joins to create the loop of the second f.

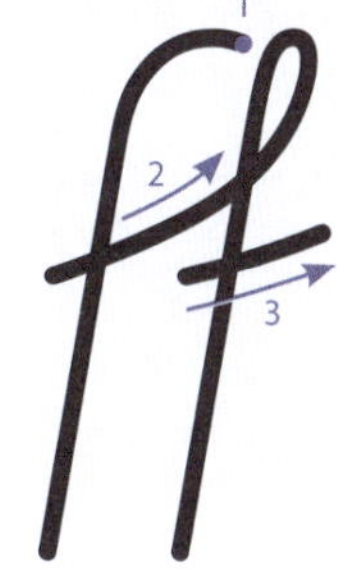

Trace and then copy these letter pairs.

dd ee ff gg ll mm nn oo

pp rr tt zz oo bb cc ss

Copy these words with double letters.

address massive keen wiggle terrestrial

sunny pool diff app worry bedazzle

valley broccoli fluff poppy bubble watt

withhold messy hiccup savvy bookkeeper

Practising tricky joins

Copy these words.

cow snow Liv lotto grow two

window potato also buffalo Gustav

Fine motor skills task: Colour in this picture. Add a caption, using words from the list above.

Trace and then copy these words.

On 16 July 1969, NASA launched Apollo 11 into space. Four days later, millions watched Neil Armstrong and "Buzz" Aldrin walk on the Moon. The third astronaut, Michael Collins, did not land on the Moon. However, the mission would not have been possible without his skills as a command module pilot.

Consolidating

Learning intention: To practise cursive handwriting

Copy the following text to practise your cursive handwriting.

Sir Isaac Newton was a famous scientist and mathematician. He explained gravity and developed the theory of colour. Newton's experiments of light and colour have contributed greatly to our world today.

Self-assessment

Assess your cursive handwriting.

- ❏ I need some more practice

- ❏ I'm making progress

- ❏ I've got it!

Assessment: More tricky joins

Copy the words below.

flew flag flint flame flood flow

Copy the qu words below.

quick quiver quarter quack quiet

Copy the words below.

potato Viv radio volcano arrow grow

Copy these words with double letters.

wiggle constellation stellar fluff valley

mission satellite wobble mass parallel

Self-assessment

Assess how you are going with tricky joins.

❑ I need some more practice

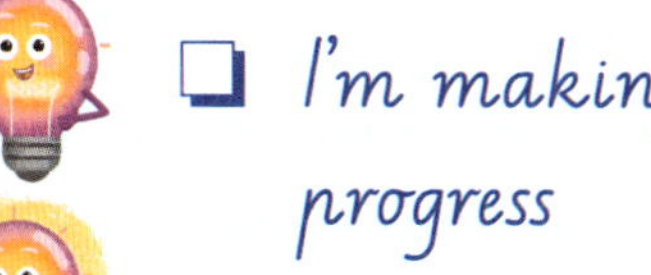

❑ I'm making progress

❑ I've got it!

Teacher comment

Handwriting hints

Letter size and spacing

Learning intention:
To focus on the size and spacing of my letters

I am successful when I can:

- ☐ check my 3Ps
- ☐ write faster using smaller lines.

Tip! Watch your horizontal joins don't go too far before connecting to the next letter.

Check your size and spacing.

not this	this
invention	invention
in nova tion	innovation
im agine	imagine

Focus on your letter size and spacing as you copy these sentences.

Marie Curie was a Polish-French physicist

and chemist who discovered polonium

and radium, and researched radioactivity.

She was the first woman to win a Nobel

prize and the first person to win two Nobel

prizes in different sciences. During World

War I, Curie realised that X-rays could

help doctors to treat injured soldiers.

Curie and her daughter Irène set up 200

radiology units, which helped to save

many lives. Her research also led to the

use of radiation to treat cancer.

Self-assessment

Assess how you are going with letter size and spacing.

❑ I need some more practice

❑ I'm making progress

❑ I've got it!

Teacher comment

Spacing between letters

Learning intention:
To focus on the size and spacing between letters

Rewrite the word "computer" with even letter spacing on the lines below.

good example — examples of what to avoid

computer computer computer computer

correct spacing — uneven spacing — not enough spacing — too much spacing

Rewrite the word "computer" with even letter spacing.

Kerning: (noun) The spacing between letters in a word.

All letters in words should be as evenly spaced as possible. This makes your writing neater and easier to read.

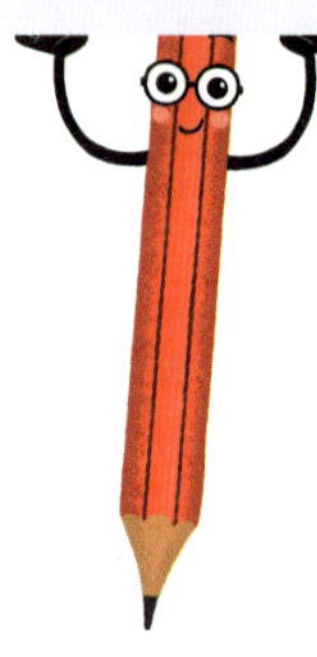

These letter pairs do not have the correct spacing. Rewrite them with the correct spacing.

ai Ld hi ck Le tt ay

wh ed ry op oo nd th

Teacher comment

Spacing between words

Learning intention:
To focus on the spacing between words

I am successful when I can:

- ❑ check my 3Ps
- ❑ make spaces even
- ❑ write letters of the same size.

Looking at these sound waves, you can see spaces. There is also a space bar on the keyboard. We need spaces in sound, in our typing and in our writing to make sense of things.

Rewrite this passage, using even spaces between the words.

When words are too close

together or too far apart, it

makes the writing difficult to read. The

spaces between words need to be even, and

letters must be of the same size.

Self-assessment

Assess how you are going with the spacing between letters and words.

❑ I need some more practice

❑ I'm making progress

❑ I've got it!

Teacher comment

Copy this passage, keeping a consistent size for your letters and even spaces between the words.

Professor Fiona Wood is a plastic surgeon
and burns specialist who lives in Perth.
Professor Wood and Marie Stoner invented
"spray-on skin". This technique was a world
first and has saved the lives of thousands
of people with severe burns. In 2005,
Fiona Wood was named
Australian of the Year.

Passport

Slope

Learning intention: To write using a slope

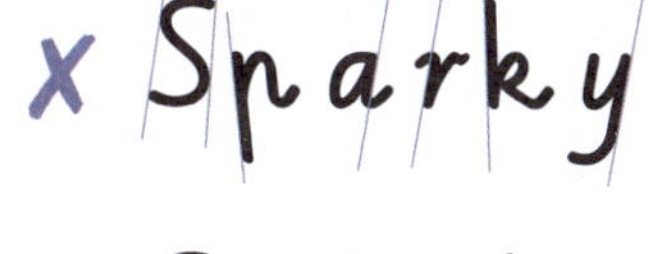

Using a consistent slope makes writing easier to read. The slope should lean slightly to the right.

Trace and then copy these fluency patterns, focusing on the slope.

Copy these words, keeping a consistent slope.

slope handwriting cursive angle direction

mountain crater stapler orbit eclipse

typewriter bicycle tilt lawnmower chess

Consolidating

Survey ten people in your class. Ask them which one of these inventions they would **not** want to give up. Use tally marks to collect your data.

Computer	Washing machine	Electric toothbrush	Video-game console

Present your information in a column graph below. Remember to label your graph.

In cursive handwriting, write two comments about the information you have gathered, such as the most or least popular invention.

1.

2.

Copy these sentences, focusing on the spacing, size and slope.

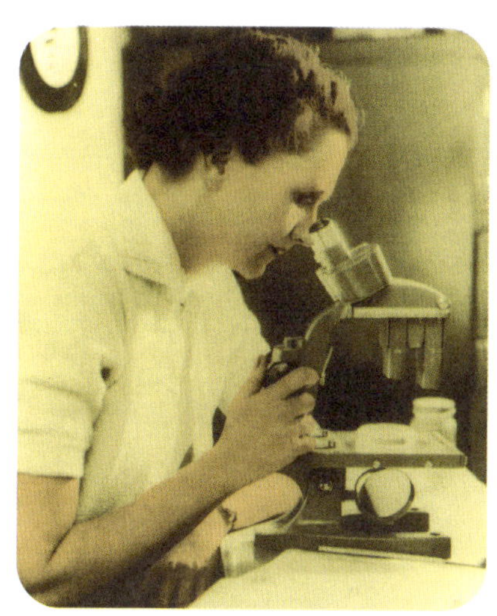

Rachel Carson was an American marine biologist and conservationist. In 1962 she wrote an influential book called "Silent Spring", which exposed the harmful effects of pesticides on the environment. She advanced the environmental movement.

Assessment: Handwriting hints

I am successful when I can:

- ❑ write my words with even spaces
- ❑ write letters with a slope
- ❑ write letters with a consistent size.

Rewrite the following sentences in cursive handwriting, using the correct spacing, size and slope.

Have you ever daydreamed about
something you'd like to build? How
would you get started? Would you
create marvellous machines, groovy
gadgets, winner wheels or awesome
aircraft? Imagine the possibilities.

Self-assessment

Assess how you are going with spacing, size and slope.

❑ I need some more practice

❑ I'm making progress

❑ I've got it!

Teacher comment

Fluency and legibility

Letters and words

Learning intention: To practise fluency

Copy the letters and sentences below to practise your fluency.

Peter practised golf every day for weeks. He

took golf lessons and practised his putting,

chipping and driving to improve his golf

and lower his handicap score. What a

great sport! Great effort Peter.

Common blends and digraphs

I am successful when I can:

- ❑ write my words neatly
- ❑ add two more words of my own with these letter combinations.

Learning intention:

To practise common blends and digraphs

Trace these common blends (letter combinations in which each letter makes a sound) and words. Copy them on the lines below and then add two more words of your own for each letter combination.

gr great green

pl plan please

nd bland grand

bl blue black

nk blank thank

spr spring sprung

squ squash squid

OXFORD UNIVERSITY PRESS

tr tree trunk

ft soft left

br bridge break

lt belt felt

thr three through

scr scrape screen

br branch brainwave

First Nations Australians cut bark from trees, without damaging the tree, to create watertight canoes (above) and the didgeridoo (right): a wind instrument made from hollowed-out trees or branches.

Trace and then copy these common digraphs and words. (A digraph is two letters that make one sound.) Then add two more words of your own for each digraph.

oa throat float

ea leaf deaf

ch reach beach

th throw think

gh laugh cough

sh ship sharp

oo pool didgeridoo

ee sheep need

ie chief brief

Let's build some words. Let's add a prefix to a base word. The first one is done for you.

prefix + word = new word

Rewrite these words, including the prefix. For example, un- + happy = unhappy.

un- happy tidy do likely

unhappy

dis- appear like able trust

re- arrange appear draw write

tri- angle cycle athlete pod

mis- place use lead understand

im- possible probable plausible

pre- historic heat view

Practising cursive writing

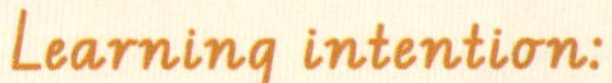

Learning intention:

To write words in cursive handwriting

Copy the two words on each line and then use both in a short sentence on the line below. The first one is done for you.

Tip! Remember that your sentences need to make sense. Try saying them out loud to check.

friends friends because because

I like my friends because we have fun.

next school

girl stopped

queen window

fish jumped

animals sun

floppy tree

everyone shouted

another way

dark suddenly

better town

think king

wish different

keep key

water fun

Self-assessment Circle your three neatest words in cursive handwriting.

Revision

Learning intention: To revise cursive handwriting

Copy the text below to practise your spacing, size and slope.

Nikola Tesla was a Serbian-American

scientist and inventor who specialised

in working with electricity. He took after

his mother, who was a scientist. Tesla

worked with Thomas Edison until they

disagreed on the type of electricity to use

for new inventions. He then started the

Tesla Electric Light Company.

Copy these sentences.

David Warren, an Australian, invented the black box flight recorder in 1954. Black box flight recorders (which are actually orange) let investigators listen to conversations and retrieve flight data recorded before a crash. This helps to prevent future accidents. In 1967, Australia made the black box mandatory.

Consolidation

Punctuation marks

Learning intention:
To write and revise punctuation marks

Edit the text below by filling in the missing letters and the correct punctuation. The words in bold are defined in the glossary that follows the text.

Louis Pasteur was born on 20 December 1822 _e was born in Dole, France _asteur was skilled in drawing and painting gaining a Bachelor of Arts degree in 1840 _his talented man was also interested in science and later gained a Bachelor of Science degree _asteur was one of the most famous **microbiologists** in history _id you know that his findings changed the world of medicine forever _asteur studied researched and then invented a whole new process where bacteria could be removed by boiling water _his became known as **pasteurisation** _n 1879 _asteur invented the first vaccine _hrough _asteur's discovery of **vaccines** thousands of people have survived fatal illnesses _n incredible innovator microbiologist artist and scientist _ouis _asteur died in 1895 _asteur once said, Science knows no country, because knowledge belongs to humanity. _is legacy changed the world

Glossary

microbiologist: an expert in microorganisms

pasteurisation: sterilisation of a product to make it safe to consume

vaccine: a substance used to produce antibodies to fight disease

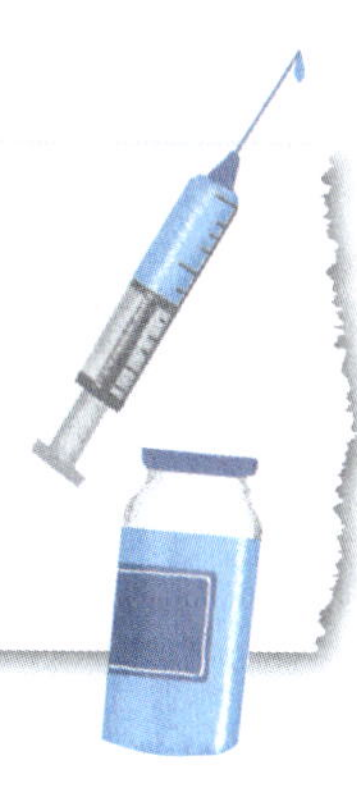

I am successful when I have included:

- ❑ 16 capital letters
- ❑ 10 full stops
- ❑ 8 commas
- ❑ 1 question mark
- ❑ 1 set of speech marks
- ❑ 1 exclamation mark.

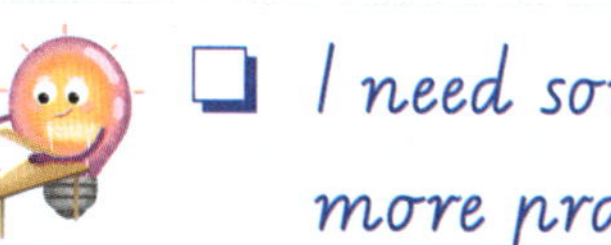

Self-assessment

Assess your punctuation marks.

❑ I need some more practice

❑ I'm making progress

❑ I've got it!

Teacher comment

Numerals

Copy these number words and then write them as numerals. The first one is done for you.

ninety-two

ninety-two 92

twelve

eighty-five

fourteen

fifty-eight

five hundred

two thousand

seventy-three

Write these numerals as words.

99

14

296

408

840

1500

Complete these number patterns.

5 10 15 20 __ __ __ __ __

3 5 7 9 __ __ __ __ __

22 33 44 55 66 77 __ __

100 150 200 250 ____ ____ ____ ____ ____

Complete the fact file about a famous inventor in this book, or you can write about another inventor that you know about.

Inventor's name:

Date of birth: ___/___/_____

Country of birth:

Invention or discovery:

Description of invention or discovery:

Timeline

You will know the answers from reading this book. (You can see the page reference in brackets at the end of each information box.)

Match the invention to the correct year on the timeline, and then complete the answer on the line provided.

The CSIRO and ________ developed technology to reduce the echo of radio waves, which allowed wifi to work. (See page 29.)

Write the name of one of the astronauts on Apollo 11, which made the first crewed landing on the Moon. (See page 35.)

This invention is used to help find out what happened when a plane crashes. (See page 55.)

This Australian of the Year specialises in burns treatments. (See page 42.)

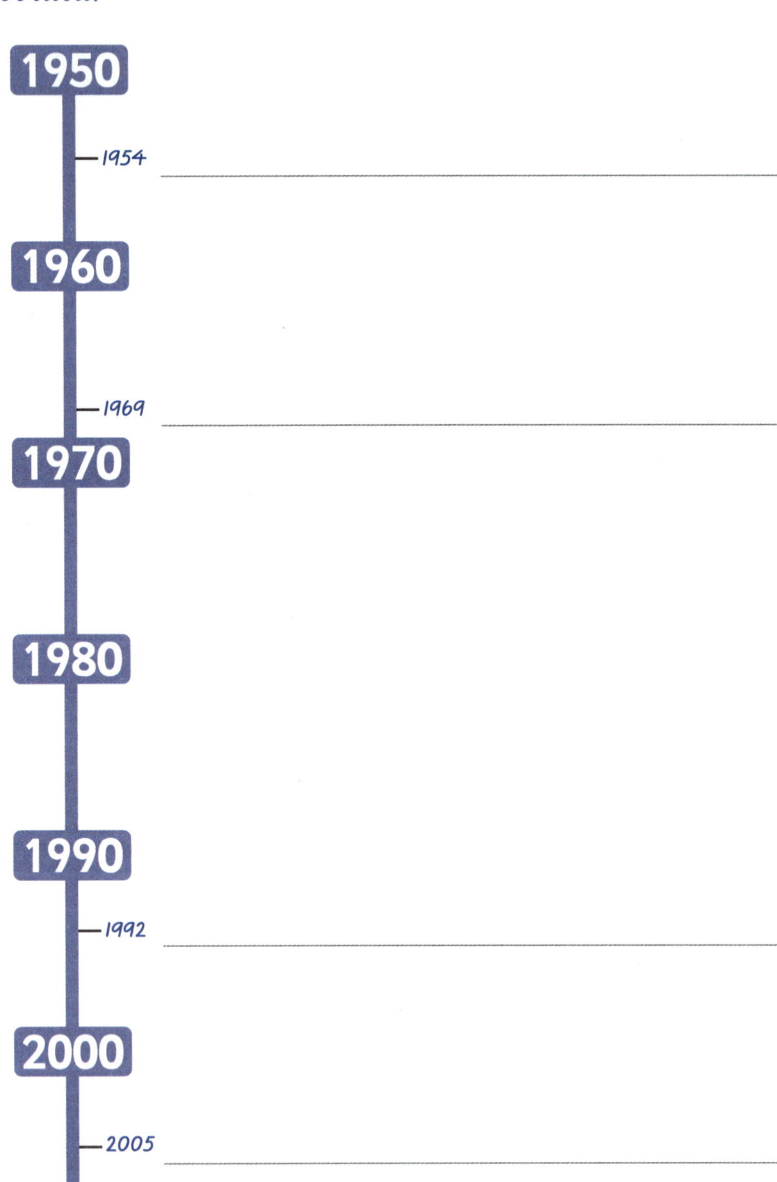

Crossword

The number in brackets following the clue is the number of letters in each word. Your teacher can see the completed crossword in the Teacher Resources on Oxford Owl. There are extra clues there as well. Try to write neatly in the middle of each square and use capital letters.

Across

3. The name for what we do when we write letters on an angle (5 letters)
5. Marie Curie conducted research on this (13 letters)
8. Something that separates words (5 letters)
9. A good _____ is important when holding a pencil. (4 letters)
10. Birth country of Louis Pasteur (6 letters)

Down

1. Someone who creates inventions (8 letters)
2. Throughout this book I have learnt ________ handwriting. (7 letters)
4. Used to take photos (6 letters)
6. Alexander Graham Bell's invention (9 letters)
7. It is important to go back over or _____ when doing horizontal joins to anti-clockwise letters. (7 letters)

Speed loops preview

Speed loops to b, h, k and l

Learning intention:
To use speed loops to increase fluency and speed when writing

What are speed loops?

Speed loops are fluid movements used to create loops and curves in the letters of a word.

Tip! The letters b, h, k and l do not need a speed loop when they appear at the start of a word.

ib oh uk ul

Practise these speed loops to b, h, k and l.

ab eb ib ob ub ah eh ih oh uh

ak ek ik ok uk al el il ol ul

table football tribe shine marathon

work think athletics tank ink well

Try not to make your speed loops too big or they will slow down your writing.

Speed loops from g, j, y and z

gi je ya zo

speed loop crosses at the baseline

Learning intention:
To use speed loops to increase fluency and speed when writing

I am successful when I can:

- ☐ sit with my back straight
- ☐ hold the pencil or pen correctly
- ☐ position my paper
- ☐ use speed loops to increase my fluency and speed.

no loop

These letters don't have a speed loop when the letter comes at the end of the word.

Practise these speed loops from g, j, y and z.

ga ge gi gl go gr ja ju ji jo

ya ye yi yo yu za ze zi zo zu

giant huge ingenuity imagination

judge jam majestic years

yellow laze zoom prize

Independent writing

Write about any of the inventors or inventions that you know of or have learnt about below. Remember to use your best cursive handwriting. You can use the new speed loops as well.